1979

A HIVE OF SOULS

Selected Poems 1968~1976
By James Hazard

THE CROSSING PRESS, Trumansburg, N.Y. 14886

ACKNOWLEDGMENTS:

Magazines: *Amalgamated Holding Company,*
Bugle American, Cream City Review,
Minnesota Review, Northeast,
Salted Feathers, Tempest,
Wisconsin Review

Books: *The Outlaw Museum Guide,*
Gunrunner Books, Milwaukee, Wis. n.d.
The Thief Of Kisses, Great Lakes
Books, 1968

Cover Drawing: Tom Parker
Cover Graphics: Karl Wolff
Photo: Susan Firer

This project is supported by a grant from the National
Endowment for the Arts in Washington, D.C., a
Federal agency.

The Crossing Press Series of Selected Poets

Library of Congress Cataloging in Publication Data

Hazard, James, 1935 -
  A hive of souls.

  I. Title.
PS3558.A887H5   811'.5'4   77-8468
ISBN 0-912278-92-7
ISBN 0-912278-93-5 pbk.

For My Teachers

CONTENTS

I

THE OUTLAW MUSEUM GUIDE

I SAW YOU DYLAN ANNE

(1948)

Yum.
Your legs are getting hairy.

My high-school-girl cousin told me that
on her mother's porch and me
not even in high school yet. She ripped
a pinch of leg hair
from just above my argyles, OUCH
I said and got the idea
girls
really go for guys who say ouch.
My cousin was also hot
to get
at me with a comb so
I'd look like Alan Ladd.

Alan Ladd, the very shrimp
who had to stand on a box dishonestly
kept out of the picture
so he could kiss Veronica Lake.
Someone told me that.

My cousin said that was bull crap
(we talked that way
in secret) and guaranteed I'd have more
S.A.
if she could get at me with a comb.
She also said shit
when she shifted.
We went for rides and she said shit
right out
when she stalled at the stop signs.
I figured her for a
whore, showed a little more leg hair,
and once we smoothed into
third
I told her the jokes I'd heard
at camp.

I'd figured her alright:
she knew every joke and a girl who did it
with guys from other
high schools.

We drove around a lot like that,
pretending
we had bad reputations.

* * *

Once my Dad wasn't at work
so we went fishing: him and my uncle
with a halfpint up front,
me in the back seat with the tackle
and my leg hair, them
singing "You Are My Sunshine" all the way
to Cedar Lake.

We stopped at Ta-too's
for worms
and beer, the men got Miller's, Orange
Crush for the kid
here, Ta-too
had bib overalls, blue-ribbed T shirt,
a Cubs cap,
and tattoos.
There was a truck company calendar
with tits.
And Sunday paper pictures of puppies
tacked on the wall.
They all told jokes there -- not
the ones I'd heard before.

I did not tell my jokes, along with
not having a beer.
But I thought the song my cousin taught me
and looked at paper cups with worms.

(to be sung)

I used to work in Chi-ca-go
I worked in a
hard-ware store,
I used to work in Chi-ca-go
I don't work there
any more.
One day a lady came in the store

I asked her what for.
Screws she said and screw I did,
so I don't work there any
more. . .

Ta-too had a hairy chin and bosoms
that slouched
under the overall bib.
When we were in the boat I asked was Ta-too
a woman
and that got a laugh.
I asked
would it say Female on Ta-too's
driver's license
                    (one time
            my cousin slipped hers out
            from the See-Thru
            plastic case and laid it
            in my hand it said
                    "F"
            for Female, I read it)
My uncle talked to me like I was younger
than he was and said Ta-too's
license would say "F", she was married
once to a dump truck
driver and he had a heart attack
leaving her a widow.

We caught a lot of sun
fish and drank
the beers and Orange Crush we brought
along. My uncle
peed
off the bow, my father off the stern,
me over the gunwale.
I started last and finished first
and left some drops near
the oarlocks.

I wanted to peek
but what you did was look straight
your way
towards the shore.

When we were done I pulled in the anchor
and we found ourselves
another spot.
The anchor came up covered with muck.

             *   *   *

The smell of
muck.

The smell of it when it is all
of a sudden in the
sun light.
It goes down so deep my father

said a full grown man
would sink in over
his head.
My hands
were covered with it, my hands
smelling like the roots of things
that come up
again
after the long-gone death
of sunken sun
fishes.
The muck blossomed
off the anchor just below
the surface
when you pulled it up to you,
the muck
glistened and shadowed in the sunlight
water.

You brought the anchor up
from the lake
then rinsed your hands in the

dark
blossom, the sunshine
dried them.

(to be sung)

The other night
dear
as I lay sleeping
I dreamt I held you
close in my
arms
but when I woke dear
I was mis-taken
please don't take
my sun
shine away

We bragged when we got home.
I helped
clean the fish with my own knife --
muck and lake blossom,
blood and guts of sun
fish
on my hands.
My mother said use Old Dutch Cleanser
on those hands.

I told my cousin
out back
after the fish fry about
Ta-too
and told her
jokes she'd never heard.
She wondered did Ta-too have periods.
(She herself did and
wore Kotex which is a sanitary
napkin: I read
the ads.)

My cousin made me promise
she could pull off
all the dead skin soon as my
fishing sunburn peeled.
                *   *   *

Pulling
in your anchor you are supposed
to slosh
the muck off it before you
bring it into the boat.
My father told me.
I spilled
muck into the boat, my father said
what did I tell you?
Sunfish spines stuck my
hands and
muck
entered me there.

My Mother said use Old Dutch Cleanser
but I disobeyed
about my hands.

That night I kept awake
my hands
close to my face, now
in the night
time the smell of all under the lake,
all that
deep enough to cover
a full grown man, all that,
close to my breathing
face: blossoming in my hands, my hands
deep
as the summer sweet lake.
I remember
myself
then, I sunk my face
into the flower

that grew on down through
the lake of my
hands to
find its hold there at the
bottom of it all,

sweet,
deeper than the sun

(1970)

which is all to say, Dylan Anne Hazard
I saw you.

I saw you, Dylan Anne, born head first from your
mother's open and opening
body, born with a splash all over
the bright table and
the doctor's hands.

You were so slippery.
I saw you, Dylan Anne.

FRANK O'HARA WAS RIGHT

Mothers of America let your kids go to the movies!
                    -- F.O'H.

The music was elegant in Indiana
(Hoosier Theatre)
& the curtains moved like night
gowns the ice was always
black
a lady skated on its

skin
of water: bare
leg curtains the wake from her nearly
silent blade & the lady's crotch
sparkling
silvery with sequins "the soul
that grows in darkness
embossed by silvery images"

Frank
        O'Hara
                was right

the lady skated to slick New York songs
on the black wet skin
& packed I knew into
those silver panties was a
You Know What
and it was dark
in there
I imagined at the Hoosier Theatre: some day
it will be like skating
on warm
black ice to fine music.

And I was right you know.

I learned it
at the
movies.

GO AHEAD, VENICE. A MIDWEST POEM.

I'm telling you this from the midwest:
Venice, go ahead.

Venice is sinking they say but they're afraid
to let it go.
One of my kids said there's a city
got covered up once by a volcano but they keep digging
it up.

Here, where I live, you can drive fast flat
out and in late summer corn is over
your head, whole households disappear
from each other till harvest.
Roads go straight, when you go
you go right on through. In Paxton, Illinois,
there's a glass round sign property
of Illinois Bell Telephone. Someone's busted the glass
out, left just the rim and you can see
right on through -- up the street
and clear out of town.

Venice, face it, you've been asking for it:

all that collecting.
Collecting and collecting, getting more
and more Venice
there in Venice. They've got so damn much Venice there
being under water's going to be a rest.
Venice,
let those stone angels and pretty pictures
go!

I'm thinking, Venice, of the vandal's hand,
full
then empty when it lets go
the stone in Paxton, Illinois.   And now
you can see
right on through, clear up the straight road.
Venice, take my advice -- go ahead.
Venice... go ahead.

THE OUTLAW MUSEUM GUIDE

What I will tell you here is one
thing. The faces.
It is the faces that I the outlaw
museum guide will tell you.
The crowd of me
I have learned to walk through carelessly.
The crowd of my faces like wild flowers I cannot name
but recognize
by fragrance or sight, familiar from other walks.

I will tell you because I have seen the afternoon
movie on Channel Eighteen, "New
Faces of 1937," and that host
was patronizing, smoothing the way back
from commercials to new faces with sappy gags
about Ann Miller & the Mad Russian.

It's a poor museum guide who puts those distances
between us and 1937's new faces.

    1. Empty.

I begin here though, with a mistake. First time
in this city I looked for the museum, found a building
with plaques for PUBLIC MUSEUM and PUBLIC LIBRARY.
It's only the library now, they've made a new
museum a block away. Only remnants of the old
one upstairs in what's just the library:
a dusty elephant in an alcove off
the children's dept.

        And an empty
case all glass, inside an earth floor scattered
with snow -- painted afternoon horizon at the back, blue;
up front the sign TIMBER WOLF and myself
reflected in the glass, standing on a Jack London
horizon, wishing on the empty case for a museum.

    2. The Cold Night.

Being a museum
goer I often recall. I recall
a winter night I lived
in a farmhouse. It snowed all

afternoon and there
was no sunset to see.   Midnight though
the clouds broke and the temperature
dropped so fast
the cold night might break everything.
I walked across the white
farmyard into the corn field feeling everything
shrink and freeze
into crystals.
And feeling crystals shrink and freeze
till they shattered
to smaller crystals, crystals small as
the day's last stray
snowflakes.

The day's last stray flakes
might be in such a cold night
crystal-frozen
bits of radio programs, that's
what I thought
and I thought if I caught
them on my
tongue
they'd melt to their sounds, my mouth
like someone skipping a radio
dial past all the programs.   What if
I caught a bit of Dylan
saying Oh
Mama
can this really
be the
I guessed my best chance lay
in lying
on my back with my mouth wide
open in the middle of my empty
Wisconsin cornfield
at midnight,
temp. minus twenty, I heard
the big barn cracking,
shrinking
to a crystal almost as big as a
barn; I kept my head
still to catch whatever fell,
snowflake
or meteorite.   The farmhouse light
in the corner of my eye.

The one flake
I got hit me in the forehead
and I got afraid
my jaws might freeze wide open. I went
back to the kitchen.

In the morning in the kitchen
my daughter saw out
to the footprints, solid now
as fossils from
midnight. "Midnight??? Wow."
My daughter looked out our kitchen window
like looking into
a museum case, I looked too.
"Wow."

We stepped into the exhibit by way
of the kitchen door and out
to the end of my trail we found a familiar
shape in the snow.
"Dad! You made an angel."

The morning after, my angel fossil.

We crunched back to the kitchen across all
that hard snow and radio
programs and my daughter agreed
it is neat to be
old,
to be first out into the snow
and leave your proof.

3. Spermic Cinema.

Angel fossil, new faces.
The angel fossil melted, and faces will.

My face melted
last spring when I was almost awake
in the morning. It softened,
the bones shifted without noise,
eyes changed color and expression as well,
what remained of this everyday
face was the pupils of these eyes, that is all.
A sad face had settled up from under,
more lined than my own and every line familiar,

19

recognized without a mirror. Then
soft as it settled the sad face faded back
to my own image again.

Angel fossils. Old faces, new faces, that instant
I had had my grandmother's face and
I think of all the faces in the bones of my everyday
face:
            new faces

of the Norman Invasion tap dancing in the lights
of my DNA, reel
after reel in the theatre of my seed
turning and turning
no commercial breaks back past New Faces
of One Million B.C. those hep cats
of the caves doo
wacka doo
turning and turning New Faces of James Hazard
whipping their jazzy little tails to that
whacked out
jitterbugging
beat
        Hey kids
    we can do the show
        here
                doo
wacka
doo

        4. Facts.

First fact, the word
museum,
used by the Greeks to designate
the home of the Muses.
        Second, Charles Willson Peale
printed on the ticket
to his Philadelphia museum
The Birds and Beasts
will teach thee. Admit
the Bearer to Peale's Museum,
containing
the wonderful works
of NATURE and the curious
works of ART.

Some customers
were scared by their ticket.

5. I Meet Her

I will be the outlaw museum guide, prophet
and publicist of my own spermic cinema
and more besides.
I'll be official with a lapel ribbon
that says OFFICIAL
and I will talk like a phony: it will be
a disguise.

I have middle aged woman, in mind.   Tall
and lean, long legs.
She's tense
and makes longer pauses than your
average museum goer, tips of her fingers
to her right cheek.
Thinking of her laugh makes me think
of a violin string
snapping
while the concertmaster plays Bartok.
It opens his cheek, like a Tiajuana switchblade.
She wears sandals.
I have dreams (within this dream) about her
thin long feet, the delicate sandal strap
crossing
the curve of her instep, then down into
between her first two toes.
Hands
of pianists, pickpockets, prestidigitators
tremble, jealous
at the grace of these feet.

She is staring and staring at a piece of meteorite
found near Redgranite, Wis.
The outlaw guide speaks to her
in an intimate yet oracular tone such as she and I
have never heard.   It is you, he says.
She is frightened.
She has beautiful feet but she is frightened
of men.   And often
she is frightened by her beautiful feet.
The outlaw museum guide points
to his official ribbon and she is less frightened.

He introduces himself falsely and soothes her
with official speech.
He is designated he says (much as angels
in other ages)
to aid
particularly shall-we-say deserving
individuals in the discovery
of shall-we
-say the
existential (ah yes) existential
import of the institution.
Now she's tense again.
Yet

she is drawn
by his intimate yet oracular tone:
Did you
know the word mu seum
(he pronounces it like an English actor
on daytime American tv)
was first used by the Greeks to designate
the home of the Muses?   Thus
our use of it constitutes a most
shall-we-say
compelling metaphor don't-you-think?
He will talk this way
because he is dreaming and because the outlaw
museum guide must have no
scruples.   He leads her
through the Man in Space exhibit, The First Americans,
Flora
and Fauna of the Prairie, (the intense bones
of her feet every step
of the way), Religion Through the Ages,
Man the Tool Maker,
the Snack Bar
where she sips frightened black coffee
and he sips
tea.

He quotes the Tao, *Before and After*
are a sequence.
He watches her feet and speaks of Evolution.
RNA
DNA
Layers of the Onion.

She's rapt.
He rips
off his official's badge and casts it
to the floor, at her
feet.

She trembles from her sandals
right on up.

      7. I Was in Leclaire, Iowa.

It's a river town, birthplace
of William F. Buffalo Bill Cody, red brick
sidewalks. The printer's window is full of antique lanterns.
In the Town Hall you find the Buffalo
Bill Cody Museum, one room without much of Bill's there
but xerox copies of letters
hustling bookings for the Wild West Show.
It's a river town, so mostly there are spy glasses,
boat models, and river pilot caps. And an anchor
hanging over head. The lady behind the desk
is old and takes donations. She points to what is in
the cases. "There's a typewriter.
From Germany." The plate on it says Stamford, Conn.
"A young couple donated it, you know." I nod.
"Found it in the attic. My sister lived
in the selfsame house twenty-five years and never
found it. But the young couple had several
children, you know, so they found it."

I buy postcard pictures of William F.
Cody and say I'll see her again.
"Well
I'm only here Fridays.
Baby sitting
I call it. Fridays I baby sit."
She flutters
her hand at the anchor
overhead.
On the postcards Buffalo Bill looks
like a river
pilot, like Samuel Clemens in fact, who achieved
fame as the writer Mark Twain.

"Spend the night here with me"
She tells him yes.

There is a buffalo stampede
on the second floor and it's chased by Indians.
One brave leaning dangerously
off his pony ready to plunge the spear,
another's horse is getting
gored
in the flank. Sound effects
of hoofs and hunting cries.

> We will hide
> till the museum is dark, we will
> make love under the danger
> of hoofs.
> Full lighting sound effects prairie soil
> beneath us.
> We will hide in the teepee
> till --

"Why don't we just wait in your office?"

She is a child, the outlaw
museum guide is bittersweet.   His foot
is suddenly bare
and across both of hers.   Her first
ecstacy, before
they are even in the teepee!
        "Trust me"
he whispers, intimate and oracular.

            (pause.)

A stampede.
The lady is calm
but now I, her outlaw guide, am frightened in my own dream.
Fantasy you know
is no fiction.   It will not be that
controlled.   It will stampede.
If there is a Muse, fantasy not fiction
is her art, and now
she is warning me of the stampede of watchmen,
of burglar alarms and electric eyes.

Arrgh.

Do I fail the test of my own fantasy??
WILL THE OUTLAW MUSEUM GUIDE CHICKEN OUT???

It is very hot this afternoon.
I have been watching the invasion of Czechoslovakia
on tv.
I had thought to go to the museum store to buy
a mounted butterfly
but it is very hot this afternoon.

8.   My Tub.

I sit on the edge of the tub
starting a cool bath,
my feet

in the water.   A slit of light
coming in the window
hits
the faucet-stream, I think the faucet
is streaming light
that shatters into bubbles
and the bubbles explode
into water.

My cool feet are deep
in that water, my ancient feet,
my long thin feet. . .

9.   I Learn Her Name.

I return to her

who wears sandals, and this is the last I will tell you
here.   A quote from a letter,
William James to his sister Alice.   13 September
1863.

>   *I work in a vast museum,*
> *at a table all alone, surrounded by skeletons*
> *of mastodons, crocodiles, and the like,*
> *with walls hung about with monsters and horrors*
> *enough to freeze the blood.*
> *But I have no fear.*

In the teepee she tells me her name is Alice.

She is afraid of nightwatchmen, burglar alarms,
Czechoslovakia, electric eyes. I,
the outlaw museum guide, tell her the letter
and how it ends "I have no fear."
We are naked under the buffalo hide.
Tonight they will arrest us.
Alice wonders
will the buffalos outside the teepee come alive
above us at midnight, like our toys
when we are asleep?
We will be trampled then, she tells me.
In the dark under the buffalo hide
the gentle cinema
of all our faces. The flowery crowd
of all her faces whispering
in one voice to all my lips. We
will be trampled then,
like the prairie,
we will be trampled like the wild flowers,

we will be trampled
but I have no fear.

THE SNAKE TREE

"All wars are boyish, and are fought by boys."
                                    -- Melville

The snake tree was a revenge --

she was old
and did not like boys, who stepped
on slender grass seeds
and shot tulips dead,
headless
with pellet guns.

In spring snakes are easily caught,
the chill
is still on them.

We boys
hiked to the marshes and our summer
swimming-hole, to cook stolen spuds
black and put on plenty
of salt. Mother
threatened us with
our death of cold and father's
hand if we should swim. We stripped
and jumped in. The ice
was gone but down in the dark
April water
there was winter.
It pained our legs and we made great
noises, then lay like snakes
in the sun, but revived
quicker than snakes --
so we caught them
all and filled the bag
my jacket
became.

A whip is alive
when you snap it. The snakes
died.

There were only buds on the branches
so we could see
clear up, through to the snakes

at the top. We climbed
at first
but boys get bored. We began
tossing snakes by handfuls
like Christmas tinsels.
More than one
dropped back down on
our heads and we were soon
sick of snakes: we did not even
stay to see
the old lady scared -- we went
to play
cops and killers, tossing
real rocks.

My brother fell
dead and bleeding at my feet.
He rose
and we walked
home cursing enemies as he
spit blood
sucked from a split knuckle.

We found our father out of breath
up the snake tree,
up high as a boy can go -- or throw.
Morons!
          Father roared.
He aimed a crooked stick
at both of us.
          It broke on the
pavement like comic-strip lightning.
               Fiends!
he shouted and jumped to the ground
to bump
our heads together.

The old lady had phoned
after
her fainting was over and father
came to get the snakes
down with a stick.

My brother
asked how he (being
we thought a bit old
for that)
had got so high in the
tree. Father
bumped our heads again.

Then before we went home
for our whipping
my brother and I took the snakes
by their tails with our finger
tips (not
sticks) to an empty lot
and buried them.
Father tried to tell us
some facts
of life but under his eye
we stamped a secret dance
on the mound and
celebrated
our breathless father, fearful
of snakes,
trembling in the tree
we had decorated.

THE THIEF OF KISSES

In an elevator today
a fragrance reminded me

of when I was a thief
of kisses.
On party nights
I watched my mother, my aunts
and cousins suddenly
as strange to me as starlets,
prettying their faces
at the dressing table.

They left fragrant dust
on the black glass top.

And I stole their red
lip
prints on tissue
to sniff

and study: I learned
those were
not movie lips my cousins
(who talked in the bathroom of their blood)
had kissed onto
the tissue.
Those prints were not
like what was left
(red as candy, after a corkscrew
squeak and pop) on Costello's
silly cheek.

Instead
there were lines of white
wrinkles in those
kisses, that made a boy look
in a way
he didn't at the movies.

(At Halloween the girls wore
sweet wax lips
that did not part, but
they were fragrant

enough to tempt a thief:
I stole
Darlene Fitzpatrick's
and ate them

like a cannibal, for wisdom.)

But the thief of kisses
learned best
what lips will teach to boys
one night when
the party was all downstairs
and he surprised
himself
with his own first kiss

as more
than a boy. He learned

the taste of black sweet glass and
the sight of his own
first dark kiss
printed like a real mouth
in the fragrant
dust
of women.

A SIMPLE MEMORIAM
FOR MY FATHER

I

Your hand stays huge
as a father's on my shoulder,
even today.
                    To this day
you turn me towards him, make
me look, make me show
you I am looking: thirty years
ago it was and too distant then,
too strange under the ball park lights,
strange then as life that bright and immediate
can be. Not close as story books
or daydreams or this
memory.

II

The light came up from the bright
outfield, up past the top
grandstand where we were, up past
the light towers over us --
the ballpark all of it rising bright
as smoke into the night-game sky.
You turned me towards him.
                              "See,"
you said, "see him -- some day
you'll say you saw him
in his first year. He'll be in the
Hall of Fame.
His name is Ted Williams."

Your thrill, then,
was beyond me. I could not, then,
imagine *Ted Williams* with him walking
right under my eyes. Your great hand aimed
me but then I did not know
I was seeing what you had aimed me
to see.

III

Now, this late, too late to say
it face-to-face, I say
to you: "Father..." (for the first time
in my life I say it, it is so simple
now) "...Father,

you were right." I say that
and I see
with your great hand on my shoulder.
It is no weight at all.

MOTHER AND SON IN A SUPERMARKET:
A UTOPIAN POEM

for Morgan Gibson

Nothing is quite right for them.
The eyes
do not find their place
in those unarranged
faces.
They take turns
pushing the clumsy wire cart
through the market
and the boy
steps
as if his old shoes were
strange to him.
I think
when he wears no shoes his
own foot is
likely as strange to him.

No one wants them here,
they move too slow.
Has some one sent them
here?
Are they to be evidence
the *retarded*
will be helped?
President Kennedy's mother
mentioned her own
retarded daughter
on tv and asked that we
be concerned: there are more of them
every year.
More and more of them
every year.

In the old days the sport
was for salesmen
with their carpetbags full
of buttons or whatever to ride the train
west and shoot at them.
Most were not good shots,
having been mainly busy
being salesmen,

but even a poor shot could
wound
a buffalo when there was
such a crowd.
And the buffalo died in the
silence
of settling dust
coughing
its own blood by the traveling
salesman's rail
road track.

The mother and son are in
a super market
but they are no good with money.
They are too slow
to be good
with money.
Perhaps they look too closely
at the pictures,
or do not look at all,
or perhaps their own hand on which
the money is laid
is too strange a sight for them
to hurry the way we do.

. . .so anyway there's this
traveling salesman and he comes up
to this farmer's house and you know
blah blah blah
and the daughter is a little
spastic or something and
she can't talk right
and that night
she's yelling like hell for
help to her father
but she says it funny, like
Farther
Farther and the salesman says
(get this)
what the hell you think I got here
girlie a. . . .

This mother and her son:
I see them as clearly as if I were
imagining.
I see they are quiet
puzzled animals
born by mistake into
humans' bodies: but you see
it gets to be that there are
only human bodies
on this earth because that is all
the hunter, man, will allow.
Year by year there are
more and more of them.
The girl at the cash register
wears a name
tag and is in a hurry to get
rid of them.

Oh I could almost wish a green country
for them,
a place where their features
might finally arrange about
what their eyes see: and where
their strange bodies
might grow
to a form that is more
comfortable for them
and perhaps even beautiful.

They might grow
huge and beautiful
as the buffalo or small
as pigeons in their own green land.
The boy's strange foot would
grow to its own
beauty and human
children would
celebrate
to find its perfect track
by a river.

A Frenchman said to THE NEW YORK TIMES:

I remember arriving in Chicago and asking people
what to see. They said the slaughter yards, which
I didn't want to see. Imagine coming to Paris and
being told that the abbatoirs were the most interesting
sight! Of course I finally took the advice but I
resented that killing animals should be the main
attraction of a city.

So
I *will* wish
their own green country

for this mother and her son, but also
I know
that country has already been --
here,
in this place.
This market is built
on its dust
and bones. Men who hunt are making
the world
so that men's bodies are the only ones
that souls such as theirs
may be born into.
And we're told that that is best.
Perhaps.
Perhaps these two are better off
in a market.
But there are days (today
is one) when I begin to grow
slow as those two
to think
that all the alternative we can offer
their souls
is the hunt or a supermarket.

The cashier's impatient with me.
I have given her too much
money
and I am slowing the line.

But there is more
to think of.
Think of it: there is earth
below this tile floor!
And (how can I know this?) a
patient Indian
is buried there. And day by day
his dust in the dust of his burial canoe
gathers itself slowly (how
do I know this?) back to its
original self, gathers
itself
slowly towards a time
when the reborn buffalo
will walk a new green land, hunterless
and growing
over the bones and dust of
traveling sales men and their super
markets and all their
Chicagos.

JOE BASS JR., SUMMER 1967

I am married and have
made two babies,
both, the boy the girl, white.
Black men are burning
Newark and Detroit.

And day after day a boy
lies in the street,
bleeding on the cover of *Life*.
He lies in not quite
the foetal way. I think
as he is bleeding (now
on my bed
room floor, silently
day after day)
I think of what is inside.

His name is Joe Bass Jr.

I think of what is inside
wounded Joe Bass Jr.
I open, and see.
Boys
and girls (blonde as my
own) on a beach
party. Quote, *Remember
the Day. . .*
In Pictures. And cops
in the pictures inside Joe Bass Jr.
do not look bright
but they've got
shot guns and yellow
helmets.
One stands by a man he has killed
while
over his shoulder back in the
picture Joe Bass Jr
is down in the street
from the same shot.

The cop has not noticed him yet.

Another quote from Kodak,
You can't capture
all the fun of the beach in one
picture, so
shoot several.

Besides the beach party there is
inside Joe Bass Jr
a picture of an elephant
with its trunk in its
ear and
a picture of Joe Bass Jr.

He is lying with his eyes open
at the foot
of a see-gar smoking
peace officer. Not
too many pages away you'll find
a turbanned sniper.

Inside black Joe Bass Jr is
the wounded
Joe Bass Jr, lying
day after day
almost like a foetus
or like a spent lover
in his own blood.

A friend of mine is frustrated
and so am I.
He says, "It doesn't matter now
if you're on their side.
With a white face you'll never join
their army. You're always out
of uniform"
I know that's true.
"So what the hell
do you
do," he wants to know.

*

What can I tell you?
Shall I come on like some quack
politician?
Shall I tell you what to do?

No
I will not tell you what to do,
but I will tell you I do
not believe in my own frustration
and I will tell you
I am not guilty
of a Newark cop's crime.
No
I'll not whack off an evening's
guilt and feel eased.
There was a day
the boy of me
took magazines to bed,
aching with babies.
Oh the sleek impossible women
of the ads --
and then
the wasted wet seed dying
in my fist like
something solid
that had melted.

No
I will not tell you what to do,
but I will tell you what I know.
I know
there is black Joe Bass Jr
inside me now, born
and giving birth
behind the bones of my white face.
I know births within
births, he
born inside me and I
born in that
birth.
I know I have made two babies,
both white
and I am finding now,
down
through my blood into
the darkest pools
of my own seed a million
black babies
to be born.

So I will not tell you what to do,
but I will tell you
about one thing.
I will tell you about my eye.
The eye of my
white face becomes, seeing
Joe Bass Jr,
the eye of my mind.
Its liquid
swimming with the faces
of my million black children,
who all begin to father
me. (My friend
Sam Grolmes
knows what you do --
he wrote
I keep my eyes open.)

So I will tell you what I know
about my eye.
The boy of me, once
with a marble in his closed mouth,
pretended it was an
eye
that could see in that
dark place.

Now tonight, my eye is on my tongue --
hard, round, not sweet;
hard, round, like a marble
like a magnum shotgun pellet in
Joe Bass's back.
I do not tell you what to do
but I tell you one thing I know.
My eye is on my tongue.

It has seen inside Joe Bass Jr,
and it sees now inside me.
It is filled with the faces of my million children,
I tell you this,
my eye is on my tongue,
it will not
melt away.

I AM THE FATHER

I thought the body part
the mother's part
was best.
But not now.

"And like all families
my father was waiting --
in an hour or so
I could see shadows."

That, from a grade-school boy
about his birth.

*

One summer morning
my children's voices

were surprised at a fog
as if it were
a first snowfall. In my bed
I heard my children
amazed
at what they could not see.

*

In my dream now
my children are lost.
I stay in one place saying their names.

Waiting
as in all families.

I am the father
waiting
in one place.
A steady shadow
and they will hear my voice.
They are holding hands
and they will see
my shadow.

I am the father.
I will say, "Here."

II

NAMING OSHKOSH

NAMING OSHKOSH

A Prose Poem - History

I.   Finding the Place

(The Menomonie Indians used the water drum in their
music, a drum part filled with water to give its sound
a voice unmistakable to people of the lakes and marshes
of the Upper Midwest.)

*

Everyone came from some other place and now all were
in the one place. The place they were was on the map,
and they read the map as their prophesy. They were men
of Destiny:

they thought that up.

The maps verified them. Rivers, mainly the Wolf, coming
down from the north of Wisconsin and ending there,
going no further. That was their luck, their Destiny:
the river could not go past where they were. It ended
in the lake Indians named Winnebago, where they were.

The logs, chopped in the north, were carried by the river
to their place. That sole arrangement made a Destiny for
them and for all the landscape around. Earth is that
vulnerable when men think up Destiny. Even rough
Wisconsin, its winters and rocks and forests, was that
feminine and vulnerable.

They named the place then. Like burial of the dead,
naming is a ritual of our deepest contradictions --
breathless possibilities of our own holiness &
a stiffening sense that whenever we want we can lie
to anyone (ourselves too) about anything. There's
power in confusing, for at least a life-time, holiness
and the lie. The worn-out place names litter our
landscapes now (New Harmony, Mt. Horeb,
Providence, Concord) like rusted-out pickup trucks.
Those trucks, driven once as if they would go on
forever.

They named this place where the sawmills would be, and a half dozen families would be rich for the first time in their family tree, Athens, Wisconsin.

The naming was done on Sunday with the available pomp. They had a preacher who knew a thing or two about the other Athens. They saw themselves as discoverers -- like the painting some had seen and all could imagine, Columbus planting a flag in the New World.

Soon some of them would be rich enough to commission that painting of themselves, from the artists who were making their way west, one step behind the namers.

(Apollinaire: *Victory will be above all to see truly into the distance to see everything up close so that everything can have a new name.*)

II. Photographing Them.

Mr. Webster was one of the namers.

He hired the men who felled the trees, he hired the men who sawed them into lumber, and he hired men who saw to the lumberjacks and the sawmill men. He was portly because that was expected if you were prosperous. But inside his bulk, like a hidden pocket-knife with a wicked sharp blade, he carried a thin Mr. Webster who talked to no one but Mrs. Webster.

*

All day along the river saw blades at work. The sound of them.

Before there weren't so many trees missing, in the hey-day, Athens had forty sawmills. You could hear them all. Some heard the blades sing through a log, some said they screamed. If you could hear the old photographs it is that sound you would find behind the eyes of Mr. Webster.

The camera men came quicker than the portrait painters. They set up the long legged camera wherever anyone said a word like Destiny, which was just about everywhere, lumber and mining towns, battlefields and railroads, Fourth of July or a public hanging. They recorded it all.

If you hear, not look at/not think how quaint, but hear those old pictures: the sound of behind Mr. Webster's eyes is in the old picture, the camera was that imperfect (honest) then.

The camera on its thin legs, the photographer in and out under the black cloth to get the composition and to discover for all time *Look at the birdie, Say cheese* -- the lens cap off to let the light in at a slow count onto the plate. It was that slow count when the light was let in that got the sound. Mr. Webster was so still, he grew thinner and thinner behind his eyes. He could not blink, or speak, or look about like a skipper checking the rigging of Athens's Destiny.

Mr. Webster sat so still you can still hear behind his eyes, the sound of a will incessant and permanent in its work as the circular sawmill blade.

There is all this arguing about who really discovered America: Columbus, the Vikings, the Lost Tribes of Israel, Norman Mailer. . . I think it was the old-time photographers who made men sit with their eyes straight for such a long slow count.

*

In an old photo of Chief Oshkosh there is no sound of saw blades. There is only almost-strangled singing. He is wearing a top hat and resembles, slightly, Gertrude Stein in an Indian pigtail wig.

The singing you hear in this old photo is the ghost song. It is the sound of every emptiness, the magic that comes if you truly despair of magic, the speech that rises when you are left in your life without language, without song, without naming. The ghost song is the echo of your disappeared life.

A bird, the red-wing who lives beside the water,
says my name seven ways
and keeps the secret of all seven in his throat.

Fat Oshkosh carries his ghost with him already
and thinks in whiskey of Columbus who found
America.

He has prepared his ghost since the Americans
named him Chief of the Bear Clan. He prepares it
with whiskey. Mute with whiskey he comes to the
ghost's songs, you hear them in the picture.

His hand me down American trousers are baggy
and now in summer you smell his shit smell
inside them. He is fat in the sun and breathing
hard, the way a drunk breathes. He wears a beaver
hat they have given him to wear. He is obedient
that way. His stomach is sick from the whiskey.
He does not walk on their wooden sidewalk, he
is not that obedient. He walks in the dusty steet
and his legs are drunk and wooden and separate
from him.

The bear went to sleep, woke, and was a man.
An Indian. He remembers that.

Now there is America. Oshkosh does not wake
up American. He wonders about Columbus and
inside him the ghost is walking on stiff legs, not
waiting for death mind you, but walking on the
dusty street inside and not needing death to be
born: he is born now, named Oshkosh, and sings
in the echo-voice of Oshkosh.

*

The Chief is talking to an American named Stink
whose nose was bitten off by a lumberjack and
who does not work in the sawmills of anywhere.
    "This Columbus, was he an American?"
    "Naw, you got it all wrong Chief. He was a
Frenchman or Eyetalian, one of them kinds. He
just come to America, he *discovered* it."

"There was America, and Columbus discovered it?"

"Naturally. . . a man can't discover what's not there, can he? This here Columbus he was a great sailor, by Jesus; so he's going to go out and discover what's there. That ain't too hard to grasp now, is it Chief?"

"Were Americans here? Before Columbus?"

"Chief, he come across the ocean in a big ship. He finds America and says I claim this for the Queen of Italy. Or France or Spain, one of them"

"Americans were there when he comes to the beach?"

"Well, there was people, in a manner of speaking, living there when Columbus arrived, but --"

"When the great sailor comes to find America for the first time, what Americans were there to see him discover?"

"Redskins."

"Only Indians? All Indians?"

"All over the place, Indians and only Indians. It was fearful for the poor man."

"If there are only Indians when Columbus discovers America, he has discovered America with no Americans."

Stink concludes the Indian has no brain for history. He drinks his whiskey and tells Chief Oshkosh to do the same. The Chief says, "If Columbus discovered America but only Indians are there and he is not American, then how can it be America with no Americans?" Stink will not answer that foolish question and resolves to drink with white men from now on, for the sake of intelligent conversation.

"The Indian is not American," the Chief says, "If the great sailor Columbus finds America, and there are no Americans there. . ."
He is no longer talking to Stink.

III.   Civilization

Mr. Webster wakes at night. He thinks, we have
subdued the erratic savage and now one working
man could kill us all.

They are talking strike in Athens. A union man
is coming from out west. Even if he is shot there
will still be talk of a strike. Mr. Webster thinks,
late at night, of all who want to kill him. Then he
thinks, I will live in a bigger house. They will build
it for me. Even if they kill me, first they will build
my bigger house.

He goes to Mrs. Webster's room, to tell her about
the house and the murderers. The house will be of
stone.

*

Going home at sunup.
I have slept somewhere from whiskey
and do not remember.
The bear slept and woke a man, I wake
in white man's clothes.
Going home at sunup I hear the crow
over the white man's roofs.
He slept, and woke a crow.

*

In a dream Joshua Slocum learned the pilot of the
Pinta guided his sloop, the Spray. Slocum was the
first man to sail around the world alone, and tells us,
"I woke much refreshed, and with the feeling that I
had been in the presence of a friend and seaman of
vast experience." He discovered he could sleep at
night and the Spray would hold course till morning.
He sailed from 24 April 1895 to 27 June 1898. In
the Strait of Magellan he discovered an island which
the charts had listed as a point of land. "I named it
Alan Eric Island, after a worthy literary friend whom
I had met in strange by-places, and I put up a sign
'Keep off the Grass' which, as discoverer, was within
my rights."

*

51

Once America was established in the river valley
they gave the Indians a second thought. What with
the houses and the sawmills built it was time for
civilization. They brought in an opera singer from
Milwaukee, they formed a city band with all the
instruments and sheet music, Mr. Ralph Waldo
Emerson (a lecturer) spoke at Fond du Lac, not
far from Athens. About the Indians, the solution
now was to have diplomacy, a foreign policy. The
Territorial Governor would send an emissary to
the Menomonie. A medal would be made with the
likeness of the Territorial Governor in profile, to
commemorate the diplomacy. Their affairs were
in such disorder it would be necessary for the
Territorial Governor to name a Chief for the
Menomonie, then he could give the Chief the medal
made in his likeness. With a Chief there would be an
occasion for the medal -- that would be the diplomacy:
they would give the Indians the new medal and the new
Chief would represent his people much in the manner
the Territorial Governor represents his. It was all working
out nicely, the Destiny. The Americans named Oshkosh
Chief of the Menomonie.

*

Columbus they tell found
America, came to it on the water
with three great boats.

This America, Oh Columbus
the deep sound
of your boat touching America;
the deep sound inside
your boat, it touches this America --

Columbus, Columbus I am a stone
falling in the sky
towards the Place, Oh Columbus its name
is the sound when we touch
the Place, the word sailing
out from our chests.

Great boat man Columbus did you hear
"America" in the deep chest of your boat?

*

NOTES ON PAYDAY

A. It is every day for a few, but on Saturday for most in Athens.

B. There are two classes of weekly wage earners: central and marginal payday participants.

C. Marginal participants take their monies home to wives or put them in the bank or hide them at home until enough money is saved to bring relatives from the old country to Athens. It is intended that such relatives also become marginal participants upon arrival.

D. Central participants do not go home. They go to the east side of Main Street.

E. The east side of Main Street provides premises, refreshments, entertainments, and co-participants for the destruction of memory.

F. Principally what is to be destroyed is the memory that one works sixteen hours a day, six days a week, in the sawmills. Destruction is achieved by means of boisterousness, intemperance, lewdness, and the eradication of one's wages -- wages, even more than fatigue, being a reminder of one's employment.

G. Marginal participants disapprove of E and F above.

H. Though destruction of memory is the deliberate aim of central participants, a vital side-effect of the payday event is the creation of memories from one Saturday to the next through the years of one's employments. The perception and recitation of this history is a continuing entertainment of paydays in Athens.

I. See "A Further Note on Payday" in Part V.

*

The half dozen families who owned Athens smiled at each other. Mr. and Mrs. Webster were planning a grand new home, there would be architects from Milwaukee and Chicago, and furniture from foreign capitals. The streets were named now, there was a school, two churches now, and some of the sawmills had begun to merge.

Theirs was no city of Destiny, they told each other. Destiny is in the future, Destiny is what you hope for: but here, now, in their city they had achieved their hopes. They were rich. What was old Athens, really, compared to this -- were they not celebrated in faraway places as The Sawdust Capital of the World?

They all, at once, discovered a desire to rename the place. An American name was what they wanted and the half dozen families who owned Athens, Wisconsin knew what American name they wanted. They all smiled at each other.

*

They are dead
I am left

They are dead
I am left

They are dead
I am left --

days like this I think
just one thing

*

The night the new, American name was decided Mr. Webster went three times from his room to his wife's, to say the name to her, to say the name city and state, over and over to her.

(Gertrude Stein: *So that is poetry really loving the name of anything.*)

IV.   The Name.

There was a Crazy Man who had secrets in the city
that would change its name. His eyes were stiff with
the secrets, even when he winked. He wore his winter
coat all the months of the year. His secrets were not
what happened to him -- he came from the old
country; that's all. The secrets were not what he had
done. . . not even what he had thought up. The word
secrets was what he had, and his eyes were stiff and
lighted by it.

He said the word, and then he had *secrets*. He had
them if he told you he did, or if he told himself.
If there was no talking, there were no secrets. Then
he cried. In his sleep, he either talked, or cried.

He kept with crowds, even if on Payday they did
things to him. In the crowds he would tell you he
had secrets when you were stretching to see over
the heads in front of you at a street fight or a
hanging. He would tell you he had secrets when
you had run into the saloon to be safe from a mad
dog in the street. He would tell you he had secrets
while you were looking up to see if it was going to
rain. He would hint his secrets involved you, or a
member of your family, while you were kicking
your horse because it was stupid about pulling
the wagon. He told you you would never force
him to reveal his secrets while you were not
looking his way and the sawmills were so loud
no one's voice could be heard.

He was a happy man. He had found his place in
the city. He was an accepted lunatic in the streets
and saloons, predictable. They all accepted that
he, like others of his sort, would one day perfect
himself: one day he might (for example) hang
himself and they would find him.

"It was his secrets," they will say.
"What secrets?" the newer ones will ask.
"Who knows. He kept them so secret."

He was born in the old country and talked with an accent. But he had found his place here, in America, in the city whose name was about to change.

*

Even the river.
The river is drunk with dead trees
and cannot say its name.

When they take all the dead trees out
for sawing them, the river is empty
and ashamed of all this mud.

*

"Music in the Menominee Manner" from LEGENDS AND TALES OF SHE-SHE-PE-KO-NAW by Beauford and Kathleen Marceil.

"The Menomonies were a pleasant, leisurely people, unpressed by time schedules except when winter chose to descend in a sudden manner! Ordinarily they had abundant time to contemplate and enjoy life. A majority of their tunes and tales were 'received in dreams', not deliberately invented by the conscious mind. Often they fasted for days to enable themselves to attain a 'suitable' song. (Note to present day composers -- when you lack an inspiring melody, just go without eating for three or four days .... Well, it's economical anyway!)"

*

Unlike the other leading ladies of the city's Society, Mrs. Webster was small bodied. She did not grow in bulk with her husband's fortune, her bosom kept tight and small regardless of how many sawmills he added to his fortune, and though acre upon acre of northern forest was added to his holdings she did not add another chin.

Small as she was, and partial as her time was to
full-blown figures, no one then would describe
Mrs. Webster as skin and bones, or tiny. She was
tightly muscled about her own center: she was,
to the other women of her city, as a fist is to a
soft hand.

She and Mr. Webster were, in a later American
usage of the word, a "couple." That is, they were
a *tactic* in their sawmill society.

*

The river, the Wolf, that carried logs south to
the city's sawmills, ends in a long and shallow
lake. It is some thirty-five miles long, six to
eight miles wide, and nowhere deeper than
twenty-one feet. The city is located about
halfway up the western edge of the lake. It
remains today a remarkably fertile lake, the
home of huge sturgeons that grow to over
one hundred pounds. In the winter the
sturgeons are speared through the ice and
prizes are awarded for the biggest fish
speared, if the catch is properly registered
with contest authorities. The fishermen sit
in shanties, outhouse shaped and with no
floor in them, that are pulled onto the ice
as soon as it is pronounced safe for automobile
traffic. The ice is the floor of the shanty and a
hole is drilled so that the fishermen can sit in
their shanties with a stove and fish comfortably
through the ice. Then the sun has been kept
out and the green life of the shallow water has
been reduced. (The lake is named "Winnebago"
a Menomonie word that translates roughly to
"stinking water" -- it is that fertile a lake.)

In the winter clear water suddenly, but slowly,
a great dark shape appears to take their minnow
bait. It is the whiskered sturgeon and he is big
as a shark. They spear him down through the
ice hole because they want to win the contest --
but moreso because they are afraid for such a
creature to be in their lake. If the spear is set
well he will fight it sometimes for over an hour

under the ice. The hole they have drilled will
have to be made wider if they are to bring him
through. The sight of him, especially if they are
alone, will make them afraid, and whatever they
have known about him, right then they will think
he is a predator. The spear will be to kill him,
not to catch him for the contest. His mouth is
not full of teeth to bite their legs off but he is
longer than they are tall, this dark creature
somehow come from the ocean and the age of
dinosaurs into their own shallow lake.

*

"I know a thing or two," said the crazy man
in his old country accent. "I know things the top
men in this city would pay plenty to know. But
my secrets are not for sale. I am that kind of man."
During a Payday he said it, when the talk was about
a strike.

*

Before the Americans came a voice from the
spirit rock had promised the Menomonie would
be protected until the boulder had crumbled
away. Oshkosh knew this was true, and that the
rock was in its place and had not crumbled when
the Americans came.

We are protected
and do not know how.

I am Chief, they have made me
Chief,

and the Menomonie are protected
but I do not know how.

Oshkosh is thinking, in whiskey, that the great
boat man Columbus could come on a ghost ship
to the shore of Winnebago. The Menomonie would
be still and the discoverer would tell them their
protection in America.

*

The scene is Mrs. Webster's room, an hour before dawn. Mr. Webster is present; the room is totally dark; they are copulating. As is their habit they converse in their marriage bed.

Mr. -- Pigs, and, Scum, and Pigs, and, Scum, and Pigs and Scum Scum Scum Scum Scum Scum. . .

Mrs. -- (*Responds with the natural sounds and actions of predators*)
UnnnghGrrRRRunghGH, etc.

Mr. -- This and This and This and This (at their) Strike Strike Strike STRIKE STRIKE STRIKE STRIKE

Mrs. -- Grr (etc.) (*She bites her husband's arm and he chokes her so his hands fill with the growlings in her throat.*)

Mr. -- They They They Theeeey. . . want want dead us dead us Dead us. . . dead dead Dead Dead Dead DEADDEADDEAD US DEAD --

(*At that moment he thinks to bite his wife's face off; Mrs. Webster is wishing that all her bones would crack simultaneously, right. . . NNNOOOOOWWWWWW!!!*)

(*Quickly, Mr. Webster rolls aside. His wife speaks first, in English now.*)

Mrs. -- If there is a strike you will crush them.

*

Another night, at the moment when Mrs. Webster customarily speaks first, she tells her husband: "I can answer your question, dear. The vote on the name will be arranged for one month from tomorrow."

*

59

EXCERPTS FROM WRITTEN HISTORIES

a.) from HISTORY OF THE CITY OF OSHKOSH
There is much in a name, and for all places as well as
persons, a pleasant name is a thing of beauty, and lives
long to bless the giver, while that which has claims
neither to beauty nor appropriateness, will live long
and like the mantle of Nemesis will ever trouble the
possessor.

b.) from OSHKOSH THE BRAVE
The place had been called Athens, then, to honor a
leading citizen [a new name] was proposed. But the
day of the vote on the name, the Indian women came
into town and, used to voting on their own tribal
matters along with men, "stuffed the ballot box",
and the city of Oshkosh, Wisconsin, got its name.
Destiny is not to be detained.

c.) from OSHKOSH: ONE HUNDRED YEARS
A CITY
A meeting was held at the house of George Wright
for the purpose of selecting a name for the
community. It is said that Mr. Evans furnished
a box of cigars, and that a little brown jug was in
evidence in the course of the meeting. The room
in the small home of George Wright was filled
with tobacco smoke, and everyone was present,
including Robert Grignon from Butte des Morts,
together with some of his Indian friends. The
group headed by Robert Grignon seemed to have
the edge on the meeting, and finally the name
"Oshkosh", the name of the Indian Chief in the
vicinity was proposed, and carried by a small
majority. The name was originally spelled
"Oskosh," and was pronounced with the
accent on the last syllable. There were quite a
number at that time who felt disappointed in
the choice of names, but by some manner the
"H" in the first syllable was added, the accent
being put on the first syllable, so that the name
was spelled "Oshkosh", and was pronounced
without the accent on the last syllable.

*

"So," says Mr. Webster, a leading citizen
of the city of Oshkosh, Wisconsin.

"So. . ." Each repetition of the word
draws the man inside him that much thinner.

"So," he says, and sharpens the blade
of himself on the stones of his new house.

*

When he had stabbed Okewa, to revenge the death
of Meshkewette, they had brought him to trial in
the court. The jury had called him "wholly Indian
in habits, character, and education and wholly
uncivilized." They would not convict him. Nor
would the judge, who said that "an erratic people"
who were sojourning with us" were not to be
considered inhabitants of the Territory. They were
not those for whom the government had been
established. There was no proof that Oshkosh had
maliciously violated the laws of the Territory and
he was found innocent.

He could understand the joke Grignon and the
Indians had made against the name that was
hoped for. But he could not understand why the
sawmill men let the name Oshkosh stand.

"They named you Chief and they are stuck
with you forever," Grignon told him.

Grignon was a white man but always said *they*.
He and Oshkosh sat with the whiskey and the
joke was better and better. "Now you are *their
Chief*": Grignon is laughing so hard he has to
hit the table with his fist. Oshkosh does not
laugh that hard, but it is a good thing to drink
whiskey with Grignon, the white man who has
lost America. To Oshkosh it seems that Grignon
is as wise from losing America as Columbus was
from discovering it. That is another joke.

"America?" says Grignon later. "There ain't
any." And Oshkosh asks him who killed all the people,
who made him Chief, who took him to the Court?
Grignon has another joke, but quieter than before:
"America. . . but there ain't any."

Oshkosh thinks, Grignon is explaining the
protection. The voice of the stone was right, and
that is the protection. There is no America. That
is the way the Menomonie are safe -- but such a
way, the Chief thinks, and takes more whiskey
with Grignon. Such a way. "Since the Americans,
there are too many jokes," he tells Grignon.
Grignon spits, and is laughing.

*

more from OSHKOSH: ONE HUNDRED YEARS
A CITY
However, the city of Oshkosh has never suffered by
reason of the choice of names, and it possesses much
native virtue by reason of the fact that it is Indian in
origin.

(End of Part IV)

A. from "Outside Fashion" by Blair Sobol, the
Village Voice, October 2, 1969. ". . . she points
out a solid beaded Moroccan belt and a beaded
vest with plain fringed armholes. Most of the
embroidery seems to be patterned after Indian
geometric designs and they discussed the whole
Indian fad. Stella cleared the subject, 'You know
this whole Indian trend stems from the renewal
of the Grand Americana -- the only authentic
history this country has.' "

B. "The stone was at the bottom of the hill and
we were alone." Final sentence of ROBERT
KENNEDY: A MEMOIR by Jack Newfield.

*

V.   Building There.

After the sixteen hour workday employees of the
Webster sawmills are transported in company
wagons to the site of Mr. Webster's new house and
they are set to building the house.

Pay for this work is not the bit of cash on
Saturday -- it is the sixteen hour workday itself.
To refuse to build Mr. Webster's house is to
disqualify oneself from employment in the sawmills.

They will work two hours nightly until the house
is built. There will be no conversation on the job
and none as the men disperse to their homes or
to the east side of Main Street. They will be hang-dog
as their great-great grandfathers were, so their
craftsmanship in another's service will be as
flawless as their great-great grandfather's was.

The thin man inside Mr. Webster will intensify.
He will come to distrust that house. Its beauty
will be too authentic.

He had planned the house as a copy, a steal from
history. That was sufficient intimidation to keep
him safe in the city that had changed its name. But
the house will grow into an authentic beauty --
authentic in the integrity of its materials (taken
by purchase from Europe), authentic in its labor.
It will grow too perfectly in the spirit of its ancient,
ruined models to be a safe fortress for Mr. Webster,
who fancies himself an American, a wrecker of the
past.

The silence and docility of the workers hardens
Mr. Webster's imagination. "The less you see,
the more is hidden," he tells Mrs. Webster. His
first and only epigram, and he is right. The
workers do keep a secret from him.

*

A labor agitator comes from the West. He makes
the house a symbol, he shames the workers, he
dares them with brutal rhetoric to Organize.
They organize and drive him from the town.

They hold their secret, they *keep* their secret.
They are building a beautiful house. That is a
fact. And they are cuckolding Mr. Webster, he
brings them in a wagon and is fat and proud, but
for two hours nightly they are cuckolding him.
They would rather have that secret than live in
the house.

Mr. Webster says more and more is hidden. He
guesses they are hiding bombs in his house. He
guesses that is the workers' deceit. The workers
keep their secret.

*

They built his house, and Mr. Webster read the
Book, especially the Psalms for they were most
murderous.

David's Song gave his soul assurance: "Arise,
O Lord; save me, O my God: for Thou hast
smitten all mine enemies upon the cheek bone;
Thou hast broken the teeth of the ungodly."
Mr. Webster paid wages to his own assassins
in a city named after a savage: "The wicked
walk on every side, when the vilest men are
exalted."

He watched them build, stone upon stone,
his house and his murder.

*

Their houses are hard.
They live in hard houses.
That is all there is to say.

*

A FURTHER NOTE ON PAYDAY

About sunup Sunday morning after a rainy night
and Main Street is a mud-stream. The rain was
warm and has made warm mud.

Those who have money left want to bet it. The
Sunday morning bet involves a table. And a card
player named Shorty, and the loudest, widest,
tallest, vastest of the ladies who live permanently
on Main Street. She is named variously, Big Shag,
Shaggie, The Shag, or just plain Shag because of
her unusual endowment below the navel. Her
Christian name is Claudia.

They lug a big table into Main Street. They are
all so drunk the lugging becomes almost as
important as the bet. Now they are not loggers,
they are luggers. They like that joke.

Shorty and Shag undress with exquisite drunken
precision once the table is in the street. They
leave their clothes on the wooden sidewalk. The
big table has settled a bit deeper in the mud on
its south side than its north, so the bet will be
done on a slant.

Shorty giggles, burps, puts one small foot over
the edge of the wood sidewalk, like testing the
temperature of a swimming hole, and the mud is
so warm he does an approximate swan dive into
the softened Main Street. Cheers all around for
that. Then, a gasp: Shag has dived in too. Everyone
thinks about that. Shorty finds Shag in the mud
and everyone yells, "No fair!" The bet was on
the table, not the mud.

Shorty and Shag are good sports. They get
themselves to the table, where the slant is
downright precarious now that she tries her
recline on it. The muddy Shag is mounting
the table and all are forgetting it is a bet. First

try, she slides off the edge and is in the mud
again -- that long instant all forget Shorty and
begin, even as the event slides before their
eyes, to remember.

Every man, even Shorty reminisces as the event
is happening: "I saw Shag all covered with mud,
her legs straight up in the air, more naked than
ever a lady was, and she slipped over the edge
of the big table back into the mud. Right out
on Main Street. I saw it"

Shorty is the last man to come to his senses and
remember there is a bet to be completed, a
performance is expected of him. He giggles, burps,
giggles again, yet his heart is not light. He has had
a realization.

Shorty has got himself drunk enough to take a dare
and end up out on Main Street naked as a jaybird,
but that drunk is too drunk, he is realizing, to do
anything at all about the dare in question. He giggles
though -- he is a good sport, he is a *good* good sport
and he burps angelically in the mud wondering what
will happen now.

Shag, the other good angel, has spread her legs
in the air again. She hollers, "Come and get it,
Sweetheart," and Shorty begins his climb. He
hopes nobody will be too disappointed when
he gets there.

Shag loses her hold on the big table, it slants
even more with Shorty there now, and they
slide together over the edge into the warm mud.
Shorty likes the mud better than the table. He
just holds on to Shag and smiles. That is when
Shag discovers her man's condition, or lack of it.
and makes the announcement to all present.
Shorty of course would never call a lady a liar;
besides, he is not wearing trousers and the mud
on his person is not enough camouflage to make

an argument possible. All applaud Shorty and
his memorable lack of condition. He and his
lady rise from the mud of Main Street and
stand hand in hand as if the bet, everything,
had been completed. In the first light of
Sunday morning the east side of Main Street
is tender, and Shorty is its tender hero. He
shrugs and burps and says (no one present
forgets these words), "How about we all go
in and have a drink instead?"

No one thinks to bring the table indoors
until Monday morning.

*

The crazy man was watching it all. He told
Mr. Webster's foreman he knew a thing or two
about that big castle they're making for Mr.
Webster. In fact, he knew more than that.

*

The Chief is talking to Grignon. His face is
sagging so, from the whiskey, it looks melted
and about to slip off the skull. His son, he tells
Grignon, is selling his land and treats his people
as if he were an American. Grignon says, "He
is." The Chief tells Grignon, "You have said
there is no America." "There ain't," Grignon
says. The Chief understands Grignon every
time they talk.

*

They take the crazy man to Mr. Webster.

The crazy man tells them as they are taking him
he knows a thing or two. He has the magic, he
can feel it. He's powerful, like Mr. Webster. He
has the secrets. "It's about time Mr. Webster and
me had a talk," he tells Mr. Webster's men.

Mr. Webster wants to know that there are secret bombs in the walls of his new house. That is what he wants the crazy man to tell him, but the crazy man just talks and talks about the power of the secrets.

"Oh, it's something, this secret. More than most could imagine."

Mr. Webster is in a hurry. "Name your price and I'll pay it."

"There's a lot more involved than money here I'll tell you, Mr. Webster. A lot more. You and me we got some thing to talk about all right."

"Does it have to do with the labor organizer? The one from out West?"

"Oh, plenty people in on this one. Believe me, this is a big one."

"Does it involve me?"

"People far and wide. I been saying all along. It's people far and wide in this one. It's a good thing we're having this pow-wow, Mr. Webster. We got plenty to say to each other."

Mr. Webster is impatient. He puts money on his desk top. "There. That's yours. Now, what is the secret?"

The crazy man looks at all that money, more than in a whole poker game. "Phew. A man with all that money, Mr. Webster, he already knows all the secrets."

Mr. Webster's man says the crazy man is just crazy.

Mr. Webster takes a revolver from the same desk drawer he took the money from. He aims it right at the crazy man's face. "Now. Tell me the secret. You can keep the money, but tell me now." But the crazy man has already said the last words he will speak in the city of Oshkosh.

His mouth is empty. He is not afraid of the gun. He knows they will not shoot him --

he is no target. It was aiming the money, not
the gun, that emptied him. But he doesn't
tell them that: he just lets them throw him
out and call him crazy and beat him up --
there was so much money they do not hurt
him when they kick him.

He leaves the city on foot and goes to another
American city, away from Athens, away from
Oshkosh, he finds another city and begins over,
empty of secrets. This time what he will tell
them, once he begins to talk again, is "I got
nothing to say. You probably think I know a
thing or two, but I got nothing to say. So don't
try and buy me off. Bigger men than you have
tried." They do not believe the crazy man and
he is never at home again in America.

*

Mr. Webster reads in the Book, "Then did I beat
them small as the dust before the wind: I did
cast them out as the dirt in the streets" and he
reads "Thou has made me the head of the heathen",
and he reads and re-reads "Then the earth shook
and trembled" and he re-reads "There went up a
smoke out of his nostrils, and fire out of his
mouth devoured: coals were kindled by it." He
closes the Book and walks up the stairs of his
new house to tell his wife what he has read and
re-read.

The dangerous stones of their new house make
Mrs. Webster flirtatious at the moment it is her
custom to speak first. "Will it always be like this,
dear," her voice is coy. Mr. Webster answers "Long
as there are the bombs." The words scrape in his
throat with the ominous sound of a boat's hull
coming to a halt on a stoney beach. His wife
smiles and tightens around her own center.

*

The statue of Oshkosh, placed in the park just
east of the pony ride, was made in Italy. The
figure is a soft, male body with a stringless bow
in one hand and the other hand's on his hip.
One foot is set before the other and he is
looking out across shallow Lake Winnebago
like a pioneer or a discoverer. That flatters the
American. Hand on its hip, the statue flirts
permanently with every history of the place, but
they are all forever too weak or too drunk to
respond.

*

from OSHKOSH: ONE HUNDRED YEARS
A CITY

CHIEF OSHKOSH DAY

In 1926 the city of Oshkosh held on May 25,
"Chief Oshkosh Day." A pageant in the form of over
200 historic floats with seven bands, was the main
feature of the celebration. The past and present of
Oshkosh was vividly shown. Following this colorful
parade at Menomonie Park, the remains of the old
Chief were laid to his final rest amid the beating of
Tom-toms of native chiefs. The grave is in front of a
large monument dedicated to Chief Oshkosh, placed
there some years ago by the generosity of Colonel
John Hicks. Ernest Oshkosh and Reginald Oshkosh,
grandsons of Chief Oshkosh, were participants in the
celebration. Princess Alice Oshkosh, a granddaughter,
was the principal speaker of the day. A large number
of Indians from Keshena Reservation were present to
participate in the festivities and the colorful celebration.
These Indians now feel the remains of their beloved
Chief can rest in a secure spot, which otherwise might
have been obliterated had the grave remained where
it was in the crude burying ground at the Reservation
at Shawano.

The removal of the remains of Chief Oshkosh
to their permanent burial place in Menomonie Park,
Oshkosh, was due to the enterprise and generosity of
Mr. Alfred Craft McComb, son of an early settler at
Green Bay, Wisconsin, in the year 1849. Mr. McComb
said that the occasion proved very educational, and
that he felt well re-paid for his expenditure of some
twelve thousand dollars, to put on the observance
and attending events. Over the remains of the old
Chief was placed a granite slab bearing the inscription,
"Chief Oshkosh, 1795-1858. A man of peace beloved
by all."

*

The land grows harder
all around me. They stiffen the earth,
they freeze it
with glass and iron, they freeze it
with their hard road and houses.

The earth hardens, like a dead water drum,
and does not know anything anymore.

I HAVE SEEN THE ELDERLY
LADIES OF WISCONSIN

I have seen them
in line to buy fragrant soaps
and I have surprised
myself:
I love their bodies.

My mind's eye has imagined
the elderly ladies of Wisconsin
all naked and the sags
of all their skins
moving like any woman's
away from heaven,

that's gravity.

I have seen the elderly ladies
of Wisconsin, their bodies
like half burned candles
dripping on the sides of bottles
secretly still full of wine
and I have asked myself

why if they buy
always the fragrant soaps
do the elderly ladies of Wisconsin
pinch their mouths so tight
about the secret of their wine?

ON A LINE BY GARY SNYDER

All the junk that goes
with being human drops away

It's ordinary.

When the junk all falls
away, nothing
seems too special any-
more. Walking through the city
a farm a forest finding
a hill
a tree for
climbing and a beach
by the lake the lake beside
the beach everything
is just ordinary.

Ordinary
as being naked, like sweet stubborn
St. Francis
walking out
of his clothes and his father's
house.

It is an ordinary thing
to be holy.
We do such extra-
ordinary things not
to be.

TO THE CARP, AND THOSE WHO HUNT HER

O, to be a dragon
-- Marianne Moore

The state sets its whole official will
against you, dredges you out
or poisons a whole chain of lakes.
They break
every assumption of preservation and they can't
make you an endangered species.
You keep on,
prolific as the poor people.

You are no fit fish for those delicate
fellows at Fish & Wild Life --
they call you. . . *rough* fish.   In China
old timers say you are the dragon's fry, the fish
of heaven.
            I've seen you in Wisconsin
moonlight rolling like little whales, playing
better than any other (except the otter)
on that lake and I've seen you bronze
backed in early morning, long and swift
with your big scales and whiskers, here-and-gone,
through the rustled pickerel weed.

And in the evening I have seen boys mostly,
or men with tattooes and good
old fashioned hair
grease, come soft-steeping it out of the forest

to stalk with bow and arrow, keeping the wake
at their shins silent as it can be. Outcasts
of the snobs of trout and fly-rods, because
with their arrows and bows they become by choice
non-casts.
           Oh, and I have watched you, fish
of heaven, here in Wisconsin, wrench
the bowmen your way as if once sent their arrows
will never stop. But, like the ancients,
a man with a tattoo bargains
for a heaven that is fierce, and once got
hard to lose. From here, on the
shore, the captured bowmen
seem more silent and ready to fly than any
men I have ever seen. They have made
themselves, fish of the fiercest
heaven, delicate water-borne kites, breathless
at the end of your willful string.

THE SOFT TABLE

The evolution is to softness says Alan Watts.
My house

softens for an instant in the morning: Susan
and I talk about rain.

The walls are soft as an animal's skin, or a plant's,
we're talking in the skin of our house.
Our house is breathing around us in the rainy morning.
When our house softens some more
we'll change the furniture.

A soft table first of all. To welcome the friends.
A soft and sturdy table for our suppers.
We'll bend it whatever way we want -- circle, rainbow
curve, or this way and that like a river.

Think of that. . . our house breathing and inside it
a soft Wabash of a table with friends
smiling at every bend like newborn river towns.

III

THE SNOW CRAZY COPYBOOK

THE SNOW CRAZY COPYBOOK

When I left the city we all were going crazy with dismay
and with wanting to blame. They had told us we could
have everything. Now we have nothing and they tell
us to keep on, loyal to them.

If we are loyal to them but crazy with wanting to
blame, we will blame no one but ourselves. They know
that. The farmers go crazy and kill their calves -- they
are blaming themselves. Everywhere, in the city and
on the farms, there is dismay. Everyone feels crazy,
blaming themselves. But I came here to the shack.

I am crazy as all the rest but I am here in the shack,
crazy on my own -- not in that crowd. Here in the
shack at least, there is no dismay. And if it goes bad
here, it will be justice (for once) to blame myself.

Winter 1934
Clam Lake, Wisconsin

1.

The sound of small dry flakes, almost pellets,
falling in a stand of cedars nearby the shack
made me strange today.

My mind jumped inside me like a stung hand.
In the cedars the dry flakes sounded like mice
bites. Yipes! I do not want to die here, is the
thought that stung me.

In the shack I was half afraid, or more, to open
the door. I might find myself laid out there,
mice nibbling on parts of my body. They have
been watching me from their sneaky corners
since I got here.

Is that why I see their mouse eyes and mouse
ears so eager in their sneaky corners? Is it me,
not scraps from my table, they are waiting for?

2.

Before I came to the shack I was like a tree in
our neighborhood park. It was a copper beech
full of blackbirds -- you could hear them inside
the cover of the leaves, stirring and chirping,
hopping from branch to branch as if they could
not make up their minds.

I was sorry for that tree, filled up inside with
a hundred silly blackbirds. I imagined all it
wanted was autumn. Leaves and blackbirds
gone, fog in its skeleton. Once I got drunk
enough to be that tree, but on fire.

The hundred birds inside me flew off with
their wings on fire.

They flew to bankers' and lawyers' houses,
perched on the roofs and burned the houses
down. One landed in a rich woman's hair and
burned her up. Some flew to their own mates.

That was being storm crazy. That would be
good, I thought in whiskey, that would end
everything. I also thought in whiskey once
of being stone crazy. Out in the flat lands
I saw a giant stone balanced on top of a
small hill. Folks in that county were afraid
of the stone because it was so old and looked
about ready to fall on them. It was ten times
as tall as a man and gave everyone bad dreams
without saying anything. That was stone
crazy -- getting so drunk on whiskey I would
feel I was that stone, standing on that hill
getting old and ruining people's dreams.

Storm crazy, stone crazy -- I learned, being
crazy in whiskey, that you can choose. With
crazy that is the good thing of it, you can
choose. Here in the shack I choose snow
crazy. . .

3.

A burning blackbird flying in the face of a
blowing snow-blizzard -- I was thinking of that
this morning.

I was walking in the very face of a storm. In the *face*
of it! My beard and eyebrows were filled with snow
when I finally reached the shack. The face of the storm,
I thought ... over and over.

If that blackbird on fire was my craziness vision, all
I could think with the snow melting from my face
was, that poor bird is a sorry sight indeed when you've
seen the real face of the storm.

4.

I have brought canned goods to the shack and
everything I can remember. Each thought falls
on each other (or on to this copybook page)
like an easy morning snow -- big wet flakes and
no wind.

The great Glacier began here just that soft -- one
snowfall on another, and another. . .

5.

What I find here is I have left nothing behind. I have
brought it all with me. Even the arguments -- I had one
about America just before I came to the shack. It was a
saloon argument and America meant politics to this
fellow drinking at my side, whereas for me it is a place
of daily life.

"I stand for America!" this fellow yells, about one
thing or another the government did supposedly to
solve our problems. I said what they, the government,
were full of and this fellow lets out a howl. "YOU
MEAN YOU THINK AMERICA IS FULL OF" the
term I used?? Now with both of us drunk -- me
drunker but him patriotic -- explanation was not
likely to succeed. I tried though. "I think the
government, not America, is full of "the stuff in
question, I explained. He asked was I a Red -- I
said no but read the handwriting on the wall.
"Anarchist? Union agitator? Nazi? Foreigner?"
No to all of those including the last, me being
born in Milwaukeee.

All present, myself included, know that he is
asking me questions till he finds an answer he can
hit me for. A crowd was gathering behind me,
looking real patriotic and the bartender was
weaseling on down to the far end of the bar and
rubbing his rag real hard on a spot where nothing
was spilled. It is also clear to all present that when
the patriotic Yahoo and I begin punching he is of
a size -- relative to yours truly -- to do as much
hitting as he wants for as long as he wants. I
figure it is best to say something that will
bring it all to an end real fast.

I take a big breath. I say, "Not only is the present
day government full of" what had been mentioned
earlier, "but the government of our forefathers was

too. In fact when he got all those boys shot to save the so-called Union, Abraham Lincoln was a first class pile of'' that.

Well there she was. It got over with real fast. Then they tossed me out the saloon door like you see in the funny papers. I remember thinking as I went out the door and over the sidewalk. (There is more time to think then than you would anticipate.) I got to thinking there that Lincoln *was* what I had said. When I said it to get the fight ended and heard it with my own ears, it was a discovery. Then, by the time I hit the street, it was a belief. Up here in the shack, I believe it still.

Such a night -- it is thundering and lightning in the middle of a snowstorm. I never did see that before -- but here I am writing about that other, in the saloon. There is the weather here, always -- but when you come to the shack you bring it all with you. Arguments and otherwise, you bring it all along to the shack and it is at least as big as the weather.

7.

The snow today was bright and frozen on the trunks of the trees. It all seemed flat to my eye, the trees so black and lined with white. You can't see the trees behind the front ones -- you have to think them up -- so what meets the eye is no different from a winter walk in a city park and today I regret I am here and not there, in the city.

If you do something, you regret you aren't doing something else.

I regret I have no more small children. When I had small children one or another would sometimes sleep with me while I listened to hotel dance bands on the radio.

Today I regret this: I regret I did not eat sauerkraut
and pork chops, I regret I am not a little drunk on
dark beer, I regret I have no fresh rye bread, and I
regret I do not have my own small child sleeping
close and the far off music close, the folks at the
far off hotel talking at their tables and moving slow
on the dance floor, faraway but close.

Just for today I regret I have the shack instead of that.

8.

I sweated in the sun splitting wood for the stove.
The sun made icicles all day on the shack. I froze in
an awful thought with the axe above my head.

What if someone came snowshoeing by and talked to me??

A trapper or an old bum wanting to talk -- or worse,
someone I knew from the city up here hunting maybe.
I brought the axe down on the block and thought,
I'd SPLIT their head and chop them up for coyote
meat.

Then I picked up the two pieces of stovewood at
either side of the chopping block and took them to
the pile with the others.

Shame, shame. Me -- Dillinger. Me -- a killer. Well,
shame on me of course but I know that the shack
and the snow, especially the snow, means keeping
this place clear of all talking until further notice.

Like I say, shame on me -- but that *was* my true
thought for the day.

9.

Lying in the dark, breathing slow, my chest growing with every breath. . .

The light was like moonlight inside the shack, but there was no moon only the snow light. I could see my table at a distance, across the shack. The fire was out and breathing was like bringing cold snow light into my chest on every breath.

I was bigger and bigger with every breath.

I was clearer and clearer with every breath in the cold light, I was like the great glacier growing and growing in the still snow light.

10.

There is a honey tree in the woods. The sun was steady all day, not taking the chill out of the air but warming whatever it touched. The smooth wood where the bark is missing was silvery and warm as spring time where the sun touched the honey tree.

The bees were out in the warm sunshine and cold air.

I recalled a tale my grandfather used to tell, that when you fall asleep your soul crawls up your throat and out your mouth in the form of a bee. It travels about and slips back in on a breath just before you wake.

There were a dozen or so bees in the sunshine. Were each souls from different people, or do some of us have more than one? Were some of those bees me? Are we different each day, depending on which bees are on the wing and which ones stay home?

If I believe Grandpa's story at all I believe most of the
bees I saw today were me. I am a honeycomb of souls.
The redskins had many gods and this fellow has many
souls, at home and on the wing, in one combination and
another changing, day by day.

11.

Not bringing a calendar was extreme. I miss the bank
calendars with the holidays, famous birthdays, and the
big treaties on them.

It's around time for Groundhog's Day by now and I
wonder about it. I always would tune in on the radio
news when I got home on Groundhog's Day. They
would tell if he saw his shadow, then explain what
it meant if he did. You had to be reminded every
year what it meant but that was all right. The best
part was getting reminded year after year.

It's a shame to miss out on that this year. It's a shame
I was such an extremist about calendars as to cheat
myself of the Groundhog and his shadow.

12.

Sitting by the wood stove, my face was so hot I thought
I was getting suntanned. Then I shivered for no good
reason, up from the middle of my back to my ears, as if
something was roughing me up.

That's what farmers and Old Country folks call "a goose
walked over your grave." In the city it's "someone walked
over your grave." Here in the shack it seems like something
else and I wonder was it a ghost moved cross my grave?
Was it grandpa's? Was it the ghost of the old glacier?

Or, I wonder, was it just a snow bee dropping on it and me
shivering so sensitive on the instant like circles on a little
pond?

13.

I walked out to the island today, which since the lake is frozen is no proper island, and daydreamed about Columbus.

I daydreamed he was in jail and Jesus came to see him. "Get out of my jail," the old Admiral was yelling at Jesus.

Jesus as usual is not taking no for an answer. He's saying real gentle, "I want to help you . . . *help* you." He is talking like a softsoaper. He is talking to Columbus like the admiral is the most important person in the world -- and at the same time, does not exist at all.

Columbus sees right through him.

"Clear out of my jail. You are too late, as usual!" My daydream is so easy to see it is like a movie. Paul Muni is the Admiral, with crazed eyes and needing a shave. Jesus is Don Ameche.

"You never were any help when I really needed it. I am a great sailor and I land in the Big House. What *good* are you?" And Jesus says, "You know I am sorry about this . . ." By now I am clear out to the island, which is about half as big as I thought it was, with a few very tall and tilting pine trees on it. I think of Columbus's masts tilting in a storm. Columbus remembers the masts too. He draws himself up ragged and proud to Don Ameche. He says, "I am ragged as a bum but I am still the Admiral -- even my jailers know that! You say you are one third of God and nobody knows for sure. I am 100% Admiral. I order you out of my jail. Shoo!"

Jesus is ashamed of himself and leaves. He has been taught a lesson by Christopher Columbus, and he knows it. The Admiral knows it too. He is proud and alone in his jail which more and more is feeling like his last great ship.

15.

I was out shouting this afternoon but in the snowfall my
voice was muffled. Like the snow was microscope animals
eating the sounds of my shouting. Later I brought in a
bucket of snow to melt for drinking water, and then drank
that brew of snow and my own voice.

16.

Towards sundown the storm broke and I went out for the
first time in two days. Snowshoeing in the wood I thought
of a poem by Emily Dickinson they had taught us in school.
The light, how it was coming across the tips of the pine trees
made me think of it.

Well, not the whole poem, just one line was all I called to
mind. It was a beaut though, so I "read" that line last night,
read it over and over and over. The more I'd read it the more
that line would mean.

So after that comes my dream last night. Emily Dickinson
and me were (it was one of those dream informations you
know without it being said) ... Emily and me were married.
We were living right here in the shack. Emily is cooking our
dinner and I am fixing a snowshoe. My left snowshoe.

She says very casually without looking away from the stove,
"You got any plans for this evening, sweetheart?" She just
keeps on looking at what she is cooking.

I keep working on the snowshoe. "Now you know," I say
very gently, "we just stay here in the shack. We live in the
shack all the time, honey."

Emily Dickinson turns to me from the stove. She has been
cooking liver and onions (our favorite). I can smell it. I put
down the snowshoe. We look at each other real soft. Any
peeping tom at the window would see, just that quick, it
is True Love between us.

"I was kinda hoping to snow shoe into town," my wife
says -- not naggy or whiney, just saying the fact -- "and
maybe sit in the saloon and watch folks play bar dice,
you and me have a shot and a beer." Emily Dickinson
is so pretty when she's wistful like that she could break
your heart.

But I have to say to her: "You _know_ I'd like that too but
we live in the shack here, Emily." She turns back to the
liver and onions, and she's not being sulky or anything.
The liver and onions now smell so fine turned brown and
golden by Emily Dickinson's small hand. The smell is
coming across the room at me, it's coming at me sort of
sad and beautiful like afternoon light. It comes to me --
and makes me so hungry I am speechless.

"Oh shoot," Emily Dickinson says, "I know you're right,
sweetheart. But you know how it is, just sitting in a saloon
with a shot and a beer. Oh come on now, and eat your
liver and onions." She dishes it out, still wistful. . . "on a
winter afternoon, I do love a saloon. . . you know how it
is, hon, it just has that certain slant of--"

I woke up right there. I almost could smell the liver and
onions. I had been sleeping on my back. My seeds were
still warm in a puddle low on my belly.

17.

Before true sundown the sun goes down behind tall pine
trees across the lake. My window looks that direction. The
light, from that time till dark, changes by the minute. Every
thing minute by minute looking new, new shadows from
things -- new shapes -- where you didn't notice the minute
before. Like looking at picture after picture, framed in my
window.

At last light, though, I wasn't watching outside anymore. My own right hand was catching the last colors coming across the lake. It was pretty-as-a-picture: the big veins on the back of it -- the knuckles -- the whole shape of it, and then looking slow all the way up my arm and down at my chest.

"This is a picture," I thought. "I am big and strong and pretty sitting here for my picture."

When all the light was gone I stayed in my place still feeling that way. Strong and pretty as all get out. I was my own favorite picture hanging on the wall with the lights out; and, I am out for a night on the town. When I get home I flip on the light and be happy to see me on the wall there. It's a real homecoming for me that way. I am glad I am right there where I can see me as soon as I open my door.

18.

I was, as I call it, "reading" Ernest Shackleton last night. His group, slogging around the South Pole and starving to death, always had the feeling there was one more to their party than the actual number -- even when the number dwindled one by one to one, Shackleton.

I saw then last night leaning into the gale and snow, pushing to the South Pole, and I realized that I have had that feeling of one more here. For many days now I have had the feeling it is not just me sitting at meals, snowshoeing, bringing in snow for water. For many days now I have had the feeling there is a ghost, the ghost of the old glacier, standing outside my door as tall as it used to be -- three miles tall.

I feel like Shackleton did about his extra explorer. I am glad for the company.

19.

I didn't expect to meet the glacier here.

But it is welcome -- oh, this is snow crazy at its finest! I
say right out loud to the great glacier, You are welcome
here at the shack. I sit at my table and I welcome the big
Papa of all snow crazy-ness to my door.

I say to myself at my table, I am here I know to welcome
the ghost. The woods and marshes and flatlands of the
great lakes middlewest are one great haunted house and
I am welcoming the ghost of the snow giant who built
it all.

This land is the castle of the snow ghost who built it all.
I hold that thought and I am happy at my table. . .

20.

I'm thinking of someone today who is imaginary and who
I would send this copy book to if I knew him.

He is a cross between Tom Edison and (as I see him) a prairie
rascal like Carl Sandburg. He is an idle man, an inventor. I
discovered I had brought his invention with me to the shack
and I used it a lot this afternoon.

If I could find him, I would send him this copy book when
winter ends. He would have known Johnny Appleseed,
would have showed him along the road. Maybe Johnny
Appleseed helped pass the invention around.

The inventor would understand the idleness of this book --
and appreciate it. Think of a man so idle he could invent
"Here is the church and here is the steeple -- open the door
and see all the people." Johnny Appleseed would have said

to him, "Inventor, it is lazy good for nothings like you and me who make the world go around." And the inventor, hearing praise for the first time in his life would agree -- "I believe you are right, Mister Appleseed. By God, I do believe you are right." Johnny Appleseed would hit the road then and leave him sitting there as usual, but now thinking proud, "What do you know about that... I have done a wonderful thing. Finally I have done a wonderful thing. Built a whole damn church with my own two hands... "

He would like that joke and his hair would fall lazy over one side of his forehead like Tom Edison's or Carl Sandburg's. He would be proud of his own two hands.

21.

God bless Bix Beiderbecke, I say. I remembered today almost all of a Bix Beiderbecke record, with Frankie Traumbaur. I danced in the shack today.

There was somebody -- Bix Beiderbecke! The way he did it, that cornet chorus on "I'm comin' Virginia," the way he just seemed to breathe it out. God bless that sweet little Iowa gin-mill kraut. He'd just breathe that song right up out of *your* chest not his!

It was finer than being drunk on whiskey, letting Bix Beiderbecke breathe a cornet solo up into my head and me dancing here in the shack in my lumberjack hat and long johns. I was dumb and awkward as ever of course, but I was smooth too -- smooth as Eleanor Powell or Fred Astaire or one of those. Bix and me.... boy oh boy....we were smooth today, here in the shack.

22.

What a storm all day today! It came out of the west
this morning and has been blowing in from Dakota
without a pause all day long. From across Dakota to
Minnesota to here -- flatland, with nothing to stop it
but some trees. The storm blows past so fast and furious
I felt like I was driving a locomotive!

Old Huey Long -- that's who I thought about today.
EVERY MAN A KING! I felt like I could yell that
out from my locomotive cab louder than the snow
storm. Good old Huey Long would have to be snow
crazy -- or *some* kind of crazy close to it -- to say
Every Man A King. Snow crazy in Louisiana is
something I'll say.

There was me sitting at my window like an engineer --
like a king! -- and the storm roaring like the shack was
highballing it through the flatlands, no stops scheduled,
ever. And Huey Long for my fireman and pal.

In the driver's seat and getting nowhere fast -- that was
me this afternoon. All I needed was the words to
"The Wabash Cannonball" to make the whole thing
perfect. What I could remember was "She climbs the
flowery mountain", but just that much of it sung over
and over made a *good* song for a locomotive snow-storm
afternoon.

23.

It is snow on snow up here and that's a fact.

All day today watching the snow makes me think, the
snowflakes dance on the wind as they fall and they bring
their dance to the slow shift of snowdrifts.

When it melts there is water and its dance. When it does not melt, there is the Glacier and its slow dance across the landscape.

Watching the big flakes fall all day I know snow crazy is to love the slow dance. I think: nothing in this life is too slow for me, my kind of show would be to sit in the good seats and watch the Glacier dance its way up and down the middlewest.

It would be so slow no one would watch it with me. It comes to that, I know. All day I watch the snowfall and all day I think just one thought: nothing in this life is too slow for me.

DRUNK IN MY HOUSE

We are inside it we are its visions we are
the spirit life of this animal: domestic
is not the opposite of wildness.

We are its visions, day and night mostly
I know it at night. Us inside it, the house,
candle's light the house crouching big
and vine covered animal at rest and us awake
or asleep in it, us the dreams in it, the long-
running animal at rest.

Domestic in my house is not the opposite of wildness.

And each house on this street in its
place, sharing the snow fall tonight: and I
have dreamed a saint ablaze in the dark
and windy spiral of heaven have dreamed him walking
towards the still center of the sea shell spiral
of heaven, so now my house dreams me, dreams me
falling drunk on the stairs of my house,
dreams me seeing one girl's face soft now
and tired from whiskey and the friends,
dreams me seeing now the vulnerable face come
beautiful in a way that is despite itself, that is
that much now itself.

                    My house dreams me
finding words for the faces of all the friends,
the friends downstairs when I am upstairs
asleep or upstairs hearing their voices.
                    My house dreams me
seeing out the front window, seeing inside
the crouching house across the street, seeing
the dancing inside there a fellow
inside there outside suddenly suddenly

on his porch doing James Brown moves on his snowy
porch, my house dreams me seeing that foolish
vision fall down the steps and roll
in the snow we all share tonight --

                              Oh, you
flipped-out Prophet house across the street!
I have seen inside you I have seen your dancing
vision fall off its own porch into the snow
and a girl come out now into the snow to roll
with the clumsy rolling dancer:

                           Prophet House,
my house dreams me seeing
inside you.

I am the vision of my dreaming house.
I am the drunken vision of this long-running
prairie animal this long runner all vine covered
in the snow. I am the vision, seeing and seen
in this wild repose, in this house that does not
come in out of the snow, in this dreaming house
that does not even stir at the dream of my drunken
face falling and all smiles
all smiles
when I think of the faces of all the friends,
all smiles to be a drunken spirit life here, foolish
and falling down the stairs
to heaven
in the wild and long running mind of my own house.